What
Falls
to
Ground

Charlotte Lit Press
Charlotte Center for Literary Arts, Inc.

PO Box 18607
Charlotte, NC 28218

charlottelit.org/press

Cover image by Vladimir Sazonov via Adobe Stock
Author photo by Amy Hart Studios

ISBN: 978-1-960558-11-4

What Falls to Ground

Poems
Lucinda Trew

CHARLOTTELIT
PRESS

*To my mother, Joan Clark Trew, for introducing me
to the wonder of words and the sacredness in all our stories.*

Contents

Grace

*"There are a thousand ways to kneel and kiss the ground;
there are a thousand ways to go home again."*

Rumi

Falling

there are riverbeds in the poplar's bark

an entire geography etched
      in furrowed hide, parched
channel, dry delta, stream turned
      to earth and seed, sapling, shade
a druid tattooed with tributaries of sky
      and of time, the inscription
of seasons, antiquity revealed
      in cottonwood veins

the best way to know trees

the best way to know trees
is in winter, without the cheat
sheet of leaves, when arbor crowns
fall to ground and all you have
are outlines against December sky

that is when you must study silhouettes
unveiled, rootstalks unearthed, seek
patterns in branches, trace the filigree of twigs
read bark like braille, understand the anatomy
of blind-folded botany

you must close your eyes, take your time
search for signs—leaf scars and catkins
the weepy treacle of sap, chestnut knob
and honey locust thorn, the black birch
scent of wintergreen in winter unadorned

when trees aren't trees at all but stark cyphers
of what they were, hieroglyphs before the fall
the cave painting aftermath of bloom and virgin
blush when what remains is a but a tangle
of seasons spent

that is how you'll know me, too
when the sun is weak, days short
when I am gnarled and bent, prettiness
long shed, brittle enough to blaze
and unafraid of standing plainly in plain sight
in this shroud of twilight wood

eve of the egg

the oblique arc of a brown egg
against a bowl's canyon rim—
this is the eve of everything

pause before the crack, the splash
the break of day when time stands still
animation suspends, and the opposites
of angles align—

convexity of shell, cupped fingers
the sloping vale of crockery—
a trinity of curvature

this is the eve of everything
before the lacquer spill
before catch and release
separating silver from gold
sun from sea

this is the eve of everything
when all is possible and mysteries
reveal a perfect meringue
or blood in the yolk

when trees fall

from natural cause—nor'easters, drought
decrepitude—they lean in, one upon another
      a prayer of knotty hands

we pray, too, in other ways, holding one another
close in crook and crutch of branch, and nests
      for those in need of cradling

we unfist fingers, unwind clocks, hold one another
in a basketweave of leaf and twig and comforting
      like trees, we slant

against wind and time, hearts and boughs that break
from storm and thorn and toppled crowns
      we ease one another

to ground, to the resting place of forest floor
to beds of moss and tender mercies yielding to ash
      as we all fall down

virgins widows and wives

~After Konrad von Hirsau 'Der Jungfrauenspiegel', c. 1200

a Benedictine monk illuminates medieval text
with portraits of women bending and tending
to the harvest of wheat, holding sickles and scythes
and shouldering sheaves—he renders them
tenderly, in malachite, ochre and verdigris

virgins
who sway in springtide breeze
green and fair-tasseled, faces rising to sun
and womanhood just begun

widows
winnowed by threshing
and the harsh drought of loss
stooping in stooks, circled by crows

and the wives
in between, ripened to gold
lying bedded and baled, sown
and harvest-grown

virgins widows and wives
who are husk and hallowed soil
wheat berry and chaff, seed cast
upon peat—they are the seasons
and a monk's circle of prayer

cello took her voice from spruce

crept into Carpathian forest
wrapped arms around trunk, cupped ear to bark
held breath, listening, for his arpeggio

from folds in her skirt, an axe emerged
newly filed and ground, blade bending to curve
as she felled the tree with concerto grace

and the earth below bowed deep
amid creak of wind, beating wings, weepy
leach of spring, vibrato of bee

cello cleaved to the wood
swooning, milling, tuning, licking sap
from lips—a forgive-me kiss

and in the end, forest sighed
in perfect time, hearing spruce rise up
from cello's throat, a rending crescendo
of timber and string

Eve knee-deep in kumquats
in the garden of temptation

Eden's floor must be strewn
with fallen fruit: guava, papaya
plantain—a taste for every craving

what drew Eve's eye to this one
this among all others, a thick-skinned
apple, stern and firm and unforgiving

why not a date or fig, pomegranate
mango—something lush and easy
on a yearning mouth

a fleshy stone fruit—apricot
or peach, permissive skin recalling
touch, ripening to blush

or olives, dark and musky
glossed with briny oil
that slicks the road to exile

berries snared from thorns—juniper
chokecherry, goji—sweet, plump
fistfuls of nectar and desire?

why then the apple
earthbound, unyielding
whose bite is like a lip-sealed kiss

whose hardness heralds
gravity and a coming, fated
fall from grace?

perhaps Eve understood
as she twisted fruit from limb
and innocence from ever-more

perhaps she knew mortality
is hard as bone and gritty core
a test requiring teeth and jaw
and the will to taste and fall

standing at the fence staring into cow eyes waiting for a sign

the steers and cows pay no mind to me
standing by the chain-post fence, staring
into their crabgrass field, into their sorghum
eyes, into the sullen sun that sets beyond
a bank of rusted trucks and tractor parts

this is where I come after my mother dies
to stand and stare and steel myself
against this broken fence
corralling broken beasts
to comfort broken me

I scan the horizon and rucked field
for signs—a ring around the pinking sun
a hymn of wind and crow
too much to ask, I expect
but perhaps—if I stand still as rye
gaze into the heifer's eyes, wait for a sign
I might just catch a heavenly herald
of crossed long horns

yet the herd just stares back
offering nothing more
than the cadenced chaw of pigweed
switching flies from doleful tails
calves who grow to yearlings
in the time it takes to mourn

the surrender of late-season spiderwebs

There is a certain time of year when the webs on my window are blowsy beautiful, a mess of silken strands spilled from peeling eaves or a Jane Austen mending basket. Stalagmites in a sunny, shutters-wide-open cave. They are silvery in the way of pewter pitchers or an old cat's whisker. Tentative, windblown and loosening, not the sturdy stuff of earlier seasons. This luminous, fall-from-grace lace is fragile now, drowsy and worn, like a dancehall girl's fishnets—torn, bedraggled and still, somehow, all the more for it. The sated sag and give, sense of *fait accompli,* the pursued and preyed upon long gone, wispily recalled. The catching, fetching days are past. Now is time for letting go—of beetle shell and dragonfly wing, of window screens and panes of glass, of solstice days and summer eves.

camouflage

on the wrong side of summer
the moth adorns screen door, pewtery
wings spread in bi-lateral symmetry

affixed to mesh like a medal of war
pinned to proud chest or cruel
spreading board

still as fossil, chalky pale, its pattern calls
to mind army fatigues, boys headed for Fort
Benning and emblems of their own

we watch for movement—
thorax pulse, flutter of fringe
the celestial pull of an overhead light

but the moth is frozen in time
standing at attention, lying in wake
and we can't look away

it is an optical illusion, cubist art
of wings, indistinguishable
from the wire weave he rests upon

then a passing shadow or slinky cat
the jangle of chimes
will rouse us from reverie

and wondering about the mystery
of moths, the frailty
of flight
we will startle, look away
leave for things in need of doing
regretting as we turn

the druid-like ruin
that found its way inside
to surrender on an August porch

the door will slam, as screen doors do—
a staccato explosion shattering calm
and turning argent wings
        to dust

Grounding

almanac

I know men who live their lives
faithful to an almanac

men who only pray
for rain, kneel in a storm
count blessings once the corn is in

men who hush women's hymns
to hearken the call of crickets
cicada and southerly wind

men who make equations
of sunrise, calculate a cobweb's
dewy spins, study the eastward sway
of a grazing cow's tail

men guided by stars and shadows
meteor showers, rings around trees
halos of frost

men who plant by the moon
harvest by tide and tithe
from weighty sacks of seed

gentle souls who've never been to sea
or church, but feel the pull within
and chart a hallowed, earthen course
to mystic springs and fields of grace

wooden spoon

cherry wood, sometimes plum
or lilac—fragrant bits of forest
he mills, planes smooth
leaving no splinters for tongue
or touch

the grain is fine
a measure of time
and trees
clouds of sifted flour
and the folding of batter
  to dough
    to bread
      to crumbs
that lead you home

he turns and trues the handle
'til it is straight, stew-sturdy
earlywood and of one piece—
Euclidean in symmetry

it must lay gentle in your hand, he says
ease against palm, cradle
in your thumb crook
fit like a familiar

and the bowl, he shows
must be carved with greatest care—
for it is a tender dip
a half-moon and a helping
a curve that cups the seasons

rest your head on cherry stones

Montmorency fruit plucked
from trees along Saginaw Bay, tossed
into baskets carrying season's stain

to kitchens, roiling pots, crimped crust
the tang of cherry mash steamed
sour and sweet, the blade-bleed

of juice that flavors dreams, pits sucked
clean of blush and meat, tucked and sewn
with embroidery thread into pillows

that clatter like castanets, fragrant
of orchard and pie, blossom and stem
and the cradlesong of prayer beads undone

the naming

I should have named him taro
the eldest, the taproot from which
all otherness stems and sprawls
like earthen veins, the rhizome of origin
bloom and stalk and family stock

I should have named him in dirt
ear to the ground, listening for breath
and tremor, the sound of ancestors
calling his name from burial mounds

I should have covered him with loam
tucked shell and nail and Solomon's seal
around flinty bed, with a lock of hair
and holly wing, witches' charms
and arms deep in clay, tilling the ground

to tend the graft and splice of this new life
I should have suckled him with mother's
milk and marrow, the compost of bone and ash
and the lore of those named before

Carolina clay

earth beneath my home-tired feet
sinks, casting footprints, shallow graves

they say it heals, this ruddy mud
that chokes my step, swallows my trail
that early clans once plastered snake bites
poulticed burns, and purified lost tainted souls
there's alchemy in this loamy mire, they claim

soothed by a potter's touch, baptized
by cleansing licks of flame, the clay transforms
caressed and tempered it holds a fine salt glaze
and cool spring water, the rain of where
we come from

parched, I crave more still
more than the earth that stains my skin
and pages, more than the blessings on my tongue
I walk on—and will my words to dry and fly
like kiln-baked wings in a cloud of dust

walking across bones

the shore tapers southward—
dunes shorn by storm
sand-storied with drift
flinty fossil remains

we walk across skeletal shards
of whelk, moon snail, auger
shark eye
carcasses of scotch bonnet
pebbles of periwinkle

shells picked clean, sun-bleached
ground to albescent dust
by the rasping churn
of surge and tide

we walk across wreckage—
exoskeletons of mollusk
crystals of aragonite
the powdery change of sand
dollars spent

our footprints are left
amid sea creature claw
and jaw, mica-bright scales
ridged back and tusk
exhumed and dredged, crushed
and fused
we walk across bones

hawk and two hares

he swaggers, a boxer circling the ring
strutting beneath poplar tree, casting
shade over the kill of two hares laid out
like toppled bowling pins—without the crash
or scoring flash of lights, without the shatter
of skeet clay, without a scream

for hares are gently made of flesh
and fur, burrow and fable, soft enough
to muffle murder, hair and hide muting
the dappled crime scene where a red-tailed
assassin presides, plumed shoulders quaking
with pride, hawk eyes dead set on the prize

taking stock

my mother goes to Italy
her last trip, she says
after the Badlands and Belize
after Europe in spring
Vancouver by sea

I organize the linen closet, fold
cloth napkins neatly, tie them
with Chianti-colored ribbon

she calls on an inter-continental
line, eerie with delay, telling me
of October light, crumbling
churches and art

she emails from the internet caffé
where she smokes, laughs
with strangers, feasts on pizza
and her Fodor's guide

I stack powder room towels
in library rows, match bed sheets
with cases, mist lavender spray
I wipe crumbs from the cutlery drawer

wash knives and spoons, return them
to their nesting bed, restoring order
seems a way not to think of destinations
far away, desire and farewells
I imagine her in lovely places
piazzas of Rome, Verona's giardinis
Palermo cathedrals, places
where relics are treasured
and ruin revered

where a woman with wild gray hair
and an inky blue atlas etched
behind her knees can stand planted
while leaves and pigeons swirl
where she can shut eyes tight
vowing never to forget

I stack cans in the pantry
sweep cobwebs from the porch
my children blink, steer wide arcs
taking stock is what I do now
I want to tell them, not to
scare them, but the veil of dust
I've stirred has done that

taking stock
is what my mother does now, too
Fare il punto
as she climbs cobbled streets, passport
and euros safe beneath her blouse
memorizing names of saints
forgiving old sins

we know the rules of taking stock
she and I: use it up, wear it out, make it do—
all fairer alternatives to doing without

copperhead

there have been more than usual this year
leafy lawn sightings and close encounters
retold on community chat boards, across
backyard fences—copperheads in the 'hood
leaving fanged gangsta signs

some say they've come for the cicadas
aged like fine cheese or wine for 17 years
a vintage the viper appreciates—he is, after all
one who can wait

tucked beneath tree stumps, sheet metal
sheds, hiding in beds of sawdust, biding time
without tell-tale rattle or hiss, camouflaged
by hourglass bands, he lingers

stretching time along the endless twine
of his spine, coiled like a spinster's braid
like Sisyphus pushing boulders, he pulls
tail to arrowhead and back again
and again, an interminable stall

and thrall, hooded eyes slouching
to dark and to dream, patiently
awaiting the heat of the prey

a poem is a bone

in the graveyard of remembering—
a bleached carcass of dreams
the sturdy scaffolding that holds
you upright, then lays you down

it is mineral and meditation
sinew and simile, a relic unearthed
it is desert skull, sand-polished
weather-pocked, where beauty

and danger reside side-by-side—
scorpion and chuparosa blooming
from calcified hollows

it is clack and whistle, a holy totem
carried off in the jaws of junkyard
dogs, retrieved again

and again from the dry riverbed
of marrow and grist, unrestful
place—the excavation of stories
and ossuary ghosts

remainderman

how did I come to be here
on this spread of low land
remainderman to stretch of pine
and sassafras, water oak and cypress
knees wading in black river?

this unexpected bequest
that is neither birthright
nor deserved—a place I never
cared for, in either sense

a place whose green to gray
ghosts haunt untilled fields
stubborn fists of cotton
and dry clay dust, the relic
bones of tractors, barns
and highway trash

I am here, the rest long gone—
I am the last remaining one
yoked by sorrel grass
and unmended fence

Grace

communion

Donnie, the tree guru who fells the broken and blighted, who has taught me to read trees by leaf and touch and what falls to ground, tells me the poplar is dying.

There is metastasizing rot, a trunk sinking into itself like the spines of old bent men. We are quiet together, faces raised to take in the enormity of stature—Heracles in boughed crown. I touch the bark, he does too, our fingers finding and fitting into the rutted, dry channels of time.

He doesn't relish the cut, the fall, life ending in an orderly epitaph of firewood. I imagine he feels what cowboys must feel shooting a lamed horse: Reluctant. Reverent. Clear-eyed in aim and intent.

When we met years ago, he asked about the scar on my chin, a faded weal I forget—so long ago. My story of a childhood fall and inelegant stitches doesn't compare to his reveal as he lifts his sweaty shirt: A lightning bolt blaze bisecting brown ribcage—a raised and knotty relic of losing his grip high in the bower of an elm, and a chainsaw that wouldn't let go.

He will return for the poplar, with an arsenal of saws, wedges, ropes—and a well-trained crew. But it will be Donnie who harnesses in, hoists himself from shade to sun, touches chest scar to bark burl—a necessary communion before the cut.

safe crossing

the churn of earth is familiar chore
to the farmer tilling field, exhuming
stumps, plowing buttonhole rows
preparing to part earth
like Moses dividing the sea
tending pasture, sowing seed
and trusting

that broken soil will knit itself whole
that rain will quench ground's yearning
thirst, that all of Egypt, or a season
can be held back by heavy hoe
strong hand, the science of tides
and tangled vine bearing the fruit
of safe crossing to the other side

if you wish to grow a garden, first seed your soul with sadness

for it helps to have an ache, a molecule
of sorrow that will swell, release and drench
the patch of earth you claim

like a weather plane sowing stingy clouds
with silver beads of iodide, lush promise of rain
something withheld—a slip of rue, a spore
of woe to bury—a slender sprig of remembering
your shallow place in all of this

a cloister of green where secrets are safe
where worm and peat, centipede and muddy
trowel will carry melancholy to the seedling
graves you dig

for a garden is forgiving – a copse confessional
a place for penance—pulling weeds, snapping
roots, kneeling in dirt

and tending, gently tending, to fragile shoot
breaching bud, those in need of holding up
and the healing grace of fresh-tilled ground

portage

If you must carry me
find a way to water
lift me to your shoulder
as you do canoes

steady me, steady you
scan the path ahead
fan your feet for root
and hitch of all that lies
beneath

listen for the whisper-breath
the sound of pending wet—
thirsty kew of sparrow-
hawk, the give of funneled
ground

read the signs of nearing
stream—rising fog, mayfly
drone, moss beard on the chin
of rock—find the unseen
spring

and when the river reveals
itself, ease me down to earth
then cup your hands that held
so well   so long   so close

drink from the veil
of watershed
and set me out to
sea

God and all the soldiers

reads the sign in a mountain town
on a curvy road that doesn't allow
for slowing down to squint, read
fine print, contemplate beatitudes
or highway bends

I drive on, passing stands
selling cider and apple butter, quilts
flapping on the porches of stores
gravelly offramps for run-away trucks
and lost souls

these roads are good for wandering
and wondering, but not turning
around—they're good for not hurrying
for pondering God and all the soldiers

his battalion of believers
warriors you watch and wait
for, expecting multitudes to rise
from foothill fog, cross the crest
shoulder to shoulder, a general
and his men

marching through mountain laurel
scrub pine, cap cloud—
now that would be a sight
to slow for and a sign
to turn around

the day was bottle-tree blue

not just the sky or lake
or side-yard hydrangea
not the fresh Yankee blue
of pre-season pinstripes

but the day itself, the plain-as-day
day, morning to amen
was blue beyond belief
if you believe in such things—

in colors and trees
with glass leaves that sun-shimmer
and sing, in prisms and spirits
cast from cobalt flasks

in the haint blue of porch ceilings
the miracle of dusty indigo hems
streets paved in sapphire
and the never-ending, bottled-up
blue of cerulean days

Sunday morning figs

when neighbors have left for church
when the whine of yard work takes a rest
when the day and all its promise has just begun
to color round the edges—and the leaf
and sun filigree of Mary's fig tree shines
pink-ripe, a sunny blush of benevolence
offering shelter and open bar to orioles
and waxwings, yellow jackets overcome
and a trio of deer made tipsy and broad-
daylight-brazen by the honied syrup
of late summer fruit that has swollen
split and spilled its grace to ground

untethered

my mother dreams of taking off
in a hot air balloon, not exactly flying
but rising, a slow-motion escape
fueled by the hiss of flame
parachute silk and her breath-
held longing to be lifted
        from ground

she collects postcards and prints
of antique airships and dirigibles
turn-of-the-century flying machines
captained by men in waistcoats
and bowler hats—she has a flight
plan of her own, a Magritte fantasy
        to disappear

from suburbia to surreal
in a swirl of sun and fringed scarf
glinting spyglass held to her eye
she will launch in a basket
packed up like a picnic
rainbow canopy overhead
she will ascend   with a whoosh

and a wave   from bumpy field
tedium to aerial parade—high-stepping
above trees and cow leas into clouds
as the earth below grows as small
        as she knows it to be

grasslands and cul-de-sac
homes, cars ferrying families
to church, bridge games
and laundry days, blackberry
bushes to pluck, gardens to weed—

        and we three
watching her float in the gondola
of a full-moon balloon, circled by birds
bon voyage cries and those on the ground
clapping leaping reaching—
'til all that remains is shadow
big and round as a basilica crown

winter sun

slanting into windows, breaking through clouds
so high-beam bright you have to look away
seek the shade of other seasons

it is otherworldly, scrubbed to a patina
that makes you listen for the overture of angels
tempting you with balmy promise that breaks

into silvery shards, frost flowers, the perfume
of oleander, a conjuring trick—leaning in
to lure you outside, mittenless and credulous

a siren call that reminds you of an ex—
trust me, tell me all your secrets
I will keep you warm

what falls to ground

it is the simplest of truths, really
all that rises, falls
Newton's apple to the head
the scissor-snip of marionette thread

meteors and acorns, single-engine
planes, airmen tumbling onto Dover
sand, gravity is when grace nose-dives
the consequence of spacetime

curling up like warped linoleum
around water stains and heavy tread
it is satellite debris spiraling in orbit
glowing butts flicked from car windows

leaving a trail of sparks speeding
through dark, it is the wisp of dandelion
thread drifting skyward with seed
and breath

held in a wish, a buoyant odds-defying
prayer that what falls to ground
rises, and that even weeds
have wings

About the Author

Lucinda Trew is a Pushcart Prize and Best of the Net nominee and recipient of *Boulevard Magazine*'s 2023 Poetry Contest for Emerging Poets. She was named a North Carolina Poetry Society poet laureate award finalist in 2021 and 2022, a Randall Jarrell Poetry Competition finalist in 2021, and a Finishing Line Press New Women's Voices Chapbook Series finalist in 2021. Her poems have been published in the *North Carolina Literary Review, storySouth, Burningword Literary Journal,* and other journals and anthologies. She lives, writes, and rambles among trees in the piney, red-clay Piedmont of North Carolina.

Acknowledgments

Thank you to the editors of the following journals, where versions of some of these poems first appeared:

Anti-Heroin Chic: 'portage,' 'when trees fall'

Bloodroot Literary Review: 'a poem is a bone'

Broad River Review: 'god and all the soldiers,' 'standing by the fence staring into cow eyes waiting for a sign' (finalist North Carolina Poet Laureate Award), 'remainderman' (finalist Ron Rash Award in Poetry)

Burningword Literary Journal: 'untethered'

Eastern Iowa Review: 'surrender of late-season spiderwebs'

Flying South: 'Carolina clay'

Fredricksburg Literary & Art Review: 'taking stock'

Glint: 'communion'

Kakalak: 'wooden spoon,' 'walking across bones,' 'virgins widows and wives,' 'eve knee-deep in kumquats in the garden of temptation' (Pushcart Prize nominee)

Litmosphere: 'camouflage'

Mersey Review: 'eve of the egg' (finalist, North Carolina State University Dorianne Laux Prize for Poetry)

Minnow Literary Review: 'winter sun'

Petigru Review: 'copperhead'

Pinesong: 'if you wish to grow a garden, first seed your soul with sadness' (2nd Place, Robert Golden Award)

RockPaperPoem: 'what falls to ground'

San Pedro River Review: 'almanac'

storySouth: 'the best way to know trees' (finalist, Randall Jarrell Poetry Contest)

Susurrus: 'rest your head on cherry stones'

Timberline Review: 'the naming'

With love and gratitude for the ever-patient, always wise souls who make writing (and life) such a grand adventure. Esteemed teachers, mentors, believers: Dannye Romine Powell, Stuart Dischell, Sally Buckner, and Mae Woods Bell. Trusted readers, allies, and cohort friends: Vivian Bikulege, John Clark, Patricia Joslin, Brooke Dwojak Lehmann, Gary Phillips, LindaVigen Phillips, Betty Ritz Rogers, Eric Sbarge, and Joe Spencer. Creative catalysts and editors extraordinaire: Kathie Collins and Paul Reali of Charlotte Lit Press. And most beloved of all, my family: Jeff, Ben, and Emma Tippett.